Maud Humphrey

MOTHER GOOSE — *Pictures by Maud Humphrey*

First published in 1891 by Fredrick A. Stokes Company

The DALMATIAN PRESS name and logo are trademarks
of Dalmatian Press, LLC, Franklin, Tennessee 37067.
No part of this book may be reproduced or copied in any form
without the written permission of Dalmatian Press.

ISBN: 1-40371-606-4 (X)
1-40371-760-5 (S)
14336

Printed in the U.S.A.

05 06 07 08 LBM 10 9 8 7 6 5 4 3 2 1

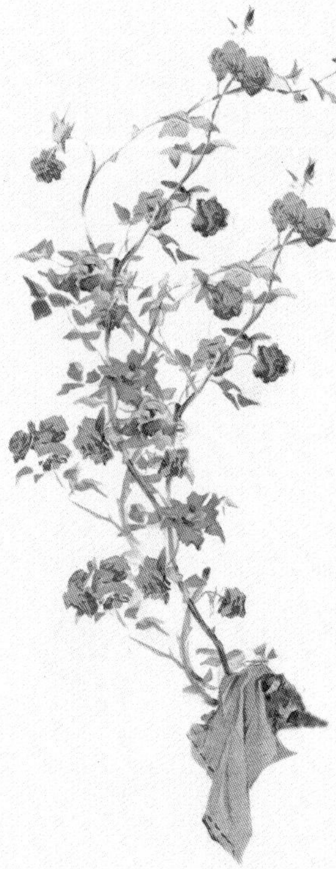

Mother Goose

pictures by Maud Humphrey

Little Bo-Peep
Has lost her sheep,
And can't tell
Where to find them.
Leave them alone,
And they'll come home,
Wagging their tails
behind them.

Little Boy Blue,
Come blow your horn.
The sheep's in the meadow,
The cow's in the corn!
Where is the little boy
minding his sheep?
Under the hay-stack,
Fast asleep!

"Pussy cat, Pussy cat,
    where have you been?"
"I've been to London
    to look at the Queen."
"Pussy cat, Pussy cat,
    what did you there?"
"I frightened a little mouse
    under the chair."

Curly-locks, Curly-locks,
Wilt thou be mine?
Thou shalt not wash dishes
Nor yet feed the swine,
But sit on a cushion
And sew a fine seam,
And feast upon strawberries,
Sugar and cream!

Ding, dong, bell.
Kitty's in the well!
Who put her in?
Little Tommy Green.
Who pulled her out?
Little Johnny Stout.
What a naughty boy was that,
To try and drown
poor kitty-cat!

As Tommy Snooks and Betsey Brooks
Were walking out one Sunday,
Said Tommy Snooks to Betsey Brooks,
"Tomorrow will be Monday."

Little Tom Tucker
Sings for his supper.
What shall he sing for?
White bread and butter.

How shall he cut it
Without e'er a knife?
How will he marry
Without e'er a wife?

Little Nancy Etticote,
In a white petticoat,
With a red nose.
The longer she stands,
The shorter she grows.

Lucy Locket lost her pocket.
Kitty Fisher found it.
There was not a penny in it,
But a ribbon 'round it.

Little Jack Horner
   Sat in a corner,
Eating a Christmas pie.
   He put in his thumb
      And pulled out a plum
And said: "What a good boy am I!"

As I was going up Primrose Hill,
Primrose Hill was dirty.
There I met a pretty miss,
And she dropped me a curtsy.

When I was a bachelor I lived by myself.
And all the bread and cheese I got
I put upon the shelf.
The rats and the mice they made
such a strife,
I was forced to go to London
to buy myself a wife.

The streets were so broad
and the lanes were so narrow,
I had to bring my wife home
on a wheel-barrow.
The wheel-barrow broke
and my wife had a fall.
Down came wheel-barrow,
Little wife
and all.

Maud Humphrey

Sing a song of sixpence,
A pocket full of rye;
Four and-twenty blackbirds
Baked in a pie.

When the pie was opened,
The birds began to sing.
Wasn't that a dainty dish
To set before the king?

Hush a bye, baby, on the tree top,
When the wind blows, the cradle will rock.
When the bough breaks, the cradle will fall;
Down tumbles baby, cradle and all.

Hot cross buns, hot cross buns!
One a penny, two a penny,
  Hot cross buns!
If your daughters don't like them,
  Give them to your sons.
One a penny, two a penny,
  Hot cross buns!

The North Wind doth blow,
and we shall have snow,
And what will poor Robin
do then?
Poor thing!

He will hop to the barn,
And to keep himself warm,
Will hide his head under
his wing.
Poor thing!

There was a little boy and a little girl
Lived in an alley.
Says the little boy to the little girl,
"Shall I, Oh! shall I?"

Says the little girl to the little boy,
"What shall we do?"
Says the little boy to the little girl,
"I will kiss you."

Mistress Mary, *
Quite contrary,
How does your garden grow?
With silver bells,
And cockle-shells,
And pretty maids
all in a row.

Little Polly Flinders
Sat among the cinders,
Warming
her pretty little toes!
Her mother came and caught her,
And spanked her little daughter,
For spoiling
her nice new clothes.

Jack and Jill
went up the hill,
To fetch a pail of water.
Jack fell down and
broke his crown,
And Jill came tumbling after!

Bobby Shaftoe's
gone to sea,
Silver buckles
on his knee.
He'll come back
and marry me—
Pretty Bobby Shaftoe.

Bobby Shaftoe's fat and fair,
Combing down his yellow
hair.
He's my love for evermore—
Pretty Bobby Shaftoe.

There was an old woman tossed up in a basket,
   Ninety times as high as the moon;
And where she was going I couldn't but ask it,
   For in her hand she carried a broom.

"Old woman, old woman, old woman", quoth I.
"Oh whither, Oh whither, Oh whither so high?"
"To sweep the cobwebs off the sky!"
"Shall I go with you?" "Aye. By-and-by."

Little Miss Muffett
 sat on a tuffet,
Eating some curds and whey.
 Along came a spider
 And sat down beside her
And frightened
 Miss Muffett
 away!

Maud Humphrey